I0605363

DREAM STATE

A COMMONPLACE BOOK

ALANA MARIE
LEVINSON-LABROSSE

THE UNNAMED PRESS
LOS ANGELES, CA

AN UNNAMED PRESS BOOK

Published in North America by the Unnamed Press.

www.unnamedpress.com

Hardcover ISBN: 978-1-961884-26-7
EBook ISBN: 978-1-961884-27-4
LCCN: 2024951911

Cover design by León Muñoz Santini
Typeset by Jaya Nicely

Manufactured in the United States of America by Sheridan

Distributed by Publishers Group West

First Edition

CONTENTS

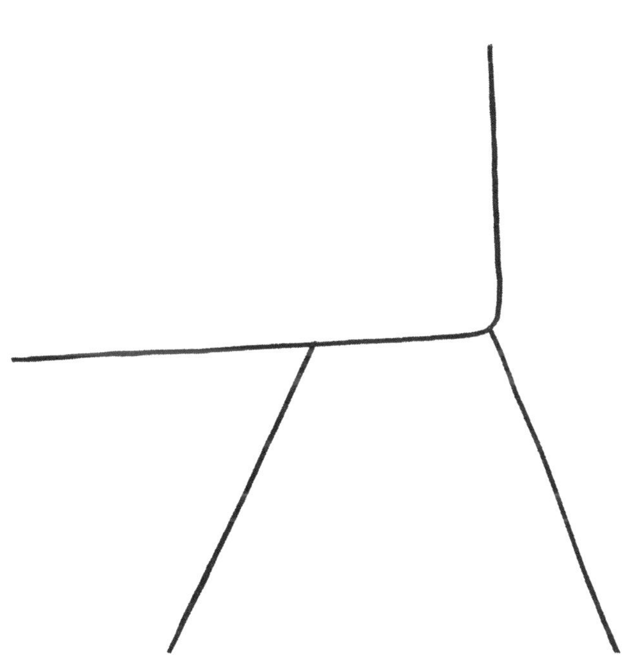

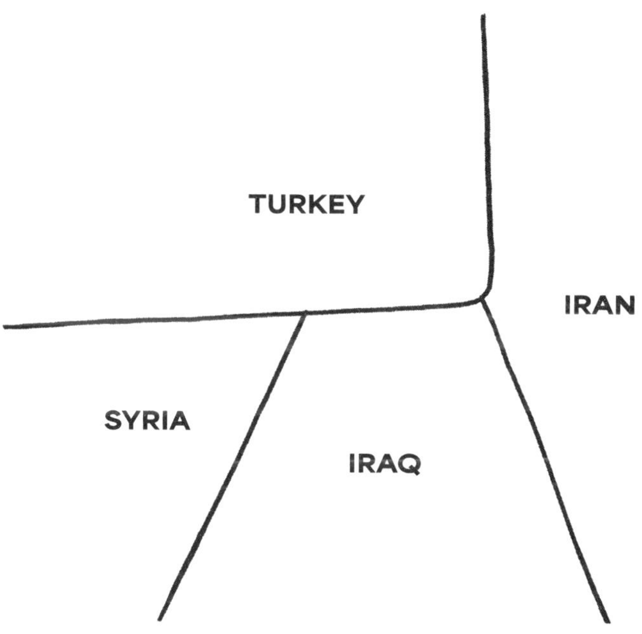
TURKEY
IRAN
SYRIA
IRAQ

KURDISTAN

DREAM STATE

A Note

Dream State incorporates excerpts from the extensive interviews I've conducted over the last decade of living and working in Iraq. As this manuscript took shape, I recognized its similarity to the regional equivalent of the commonplace book, the *kashkul*, which takes its name from the peripatetic Sufi dervish's begging bowl. Visually distinguished by typography, the speakers in my *kashkul* have graciously agreed to have their voices included here, and I have provided biographies for each speaker at the end of this volume.

No one lives now where I did. It's all destroyed. The bridges, the cinema, the library. We didn't know, but they doused the books with accelerant. Anyone who threw water at the fire only made the books burn faster.

When I was growing up, Mosul was a mosaic. Now, it is simple tile. But every Iraqi has a sad story. Kuwait. The Iraq War. I'm not unusual. I'm happy I finished university, the only person in my village who did.

Mustafa Hamdun, my skinny English teacher, used to say, *A full belly means an empty brain*. Today, we eat and eat, we see only how much we eat, not whether it is good. We only eat.

When I was ten years old, my father's friend came to visit. There were no buses, no cars. People walked. Our friend came at night. Wolves attacked him. He climbed a tree and stayed there all night. In the morning, the wolves dispersed, and he climbed down and kept walking. My father said, *Life is precious!* His friend took us to see the tree. We looked up into the branches, and my father's friend said, *That's where I slept. Life is precious.*

This is a story we told. But also it happened.

—Majid
Khazir Camp, Mosul Province

The Book Men

for Mohammed Ali Qaradaghi

As I read and work
to understand,
the book men watch.
They decide
when and how
to give me the next
book. It is easy to remember
I work in darkness
and read only scraps.

Sense is an illusion
that sometimes
shimmers and
dissipates. In the darkness
I hear echoes
that speak the great space
around me.

The book men have been
jailed and beaten
for their libraries,
used as evidence at trial,
then burned.
They asked that books
be their payment
for delivering the unsteady calf
or a Friday sermon. They read
as they went blind and after
whatever they had

learned by heart.
Cities were gassed,
the language outlawed.
Families splintered.
What scraps were found
the book men sewed
into new bindings.
Context was lost
and made and
the words lived
on even, perhaps only,
in misunderstanding.
In some ways, it is better
to be forgotten. To work
in the dark is to truly work.

The book men keep their catalogs
secret. A catalog can be a checklist:
What is left to sell? Burn? Prosecute?

So, the book men watch
me: to see what I do
with each revelation, to see
if I merit the next words.
They wait to see
what I can become.

There is no Kurdish nation except
in the manuscripts we have. Berlin,
Baghdad, London, Istanbul: each city tells us
the story of where history has taken our culture.
One book references another. Back and back and
back we go.

I began collecting in 1970.
I was married in 1971.
My son was born in 1972.
My first book was published in 1973.
In 1976, the Republican Guard confiscated what I'd collected.
Anthologies of poetry were criminal evidence
against me in my trial. Of the jail's possessions,
human beings were cheapest.
I thought of nothing. Of course
I expected death. Many experienced worse.
The sentence eventually handed down
was for six months' imprisonment.
I'd already served nine.
They let me go. They owe
me three months.

I returned immediately
to collecting, warmer
to the work. Now, I keep
the books secret.
At times, I split up
the library between locations.

There is no income. It is hard work. I preached
as a mullah, first in Baghdad, then here in Slemani.
I trade sermons for manuscripts. People gift me papers,
asking me only to analyze and publish. I have written
forty books, more than seventy volumes.

If I sense spirit in a young person, I push them
to pursue the work. I have started a revolution
this way, a revolution that is more difficult
than the political. It is easy
to stand on television and say,
We are Kurds! It is difficult to find a vision
of what *Kurd* means. Sincerity
must drive the work. Yes, it weighs on me.
The work is too heavy. I carry it only
by the prayers of my teacher, Sheikh Abdul-Karim.
He told me, *You are the past's tongue.*
He gave me permission
to teach. He taught my son. In this house,
when we say *teacher*, we mean only
Sheikh Abdul-Karim.

When Daesh pushed on Hawler, we prayed,
Please, God, don't will this. We've been
digitizing our archive for fifteen years.
My son wrote the first Kurdish font for an IBM.
There are hundreds and hundreds
of manuscripts now. We could not leave them.

That is a goat's skin. My
son's friend inscribed it for us.
It is a verse from the Qur'an,
All I am, all I have,
is a gift from God.

—Mohammed Ali Qaradaghi
Slemani

Now it is difficult for me to bring people to the soul
world. Islamic radicals make it difficult. They say this
is right, this is wrong. They fuck our minds. No one
who holds truth tortures people with it. Which is
the wrong Islam? That which pits its believers against
all else. Inside these walls, we talk about knowledge,
knowledge of God. If you know God, you can know
anyone. If you don't know God, you know no one.

You, a stranger, a woman of a different religion, come here to me.
Some would criticize me, *How can you let her in here?* But the truth
is that you and I deal in creation, God's creation. I confront you as a diamond
of God. A prayer bead at rest is in worship. A Persian poet says, *No matter*
my location, I pray facing the wall. You are my only intention. You, a stranger,
you came through the invitation of the Sheikh, but the purpose of your
    visit is this
writing: knowledge.

The basis of this work is intent.

What's the difference between this Sufism and that?
A math teacher in one city teaches with these techniques,
in another city, with those. Both teach mathematics. The text
is the same. You, stranger, are not like us, you read anything.
You dive deep. In the great world of vision, you see only God.

This road tells us I can do nothing *to* you. You must place your desires
under your feet. I ask, *How can I come to you?* The road says,
Place your desires under your feet.

I have not answered any calling. I sit and I serve.

Nothing is transactional. As the Mother of the Good said, *I will*
douse the fires of hell and burn paradise to the ground so
no one will love God for fear or ambition. We don't give
ijaza, permission to teach, just to keep the bazaar crowded.
Our grandfathers were servants of this place, servants of
Kirkuk, servants. A servant can learn.

Young people here have no
understanding. They marry, but mistreat their wives.
In our Friday sermons, we teach them to be warm, soft,
kind. Preaching must give something to the heart.

None of this is mine. The river appears and flows over us. The river is like this.

How many prophets have we had? What have they taught
us? Travel. Be brave. Learn. Be generous. An early sheikh
in this tekiye's history, Sheikh Abdulrahman, was walking through
a bazaar. He heard a santur. He became possessed. He danced. His father
was furious. *How can you dance and worship in a place where*
people drink wine? Sheikh Abdulrahman said, *If you desire*
to see God, you put your feet onto his ground without asking

a thing. We have invited the scholars of Sharia here.
They won't come. They call us different names. We don't
care. We serve them. We feed them. Good food. Even
as they eat, they call us names. Sufism is more than sentences.

I like this talk. It is outside our world.

—Sheikh Yusuf Talabani
Talabani Tekiye, Kirkuk

Living

He said: If you can't make or steal
a living elsewhere, become
a poet, one of four hundred
under the King of Poets.

This is not a world
my desires dreamed up.

This is country
my country has
burned down.

In 2003, you know, we were excited to lose Saddam. We thought America would make us a great country. We thought we would be able to travel on our passports, freely, like Americans. That we would be able to kiss a girl on the street. I mean, we were teenagers and this is what we thought.

The news was so slow, a month behind, and not every family had a TV. I wanted to see what was going on in my hometown, Kirkuk. Curious, as always, I walked there. I wish I had been a photographer at that time.

In 2003, Kirkuk was only half liberated. Only Chamchamali crazy dudes and military transports drove the Kirkuk road then. The soldiers allowed only trucks into the city, no cars, so people would smuggle themselves, just like now, and run out of oxygen and die. Too, soldiers, mad at oil smugglers or just bored, would throw fire into the backs of trucks. I watched people burn this way. No one cared. Sure, they were civilians, but they were Kurds.

—Hawre Khalid
Slemani

After 2003, Kurdistan opened to America, the West, so what do new things mean? It's not easy to say. Freedom was new. Talking Kurdish was new. Murakami, Kundera, Borges: I read a lot.

Before I began to translate I was just like any other reader, sitting at home and reading, but then, when my English was good enough, I thought, *Halo, don't be selfish.* It's selfish to sit at home and do what you love. So, I started translating. To give others the chance to read these great novels.

Training as a soldier didn't make me who I am. It made me stronger. But books made me who I am. Books make me a human being again. They open my mind wide. Before books I didn't know the whole world. Media says what it wants. The true world is not in TV, screens, social media. It's out there. Out there. Books give us the true world. I read and translate on the battlefield. When I have a cabin or tent, I translate. When I don't, I go under the truck and read. There's no shadow, no breath, except under the car.

The Islamic State dies for paradise. YPG dies for their homeland. Both sides have nothing to lose. So, these battles have been like nothing I've seen. This is hard to say, especially on camera, but I've wept for the Islamic State. I see them as victims, victims of political ideas, as pesh merga are: victims.

After each attack, when you're a commander, you have so much to do. Reorder rockets, clean the weapons. I give my men their tasks. I go to my cabin. I lock the door. I weep. I joined to help. All I've ever wanted is to help. That's why I joined. I don't know what we're doing anymore.

I deal with death on the battlefield, but I don't work for death. I work for life. The more you think about God and heaven, the less you think about humanity. My religion is to look down, not up.

I stopped praying my first week in the battlefield fighting ISIS. When pesh merga launch a rocket, they say, *Allahu Akbar*. When the Hashd launch a rocket, they say, *Allahu Akbar*. I agree. God is great. But for whom?

The work I do, that's my prayer now. Even my rest is in my work. You don't need to sit and pray for what we've lost, what we're about to lose. So much remains.

—Halo Fariq
Slemani

A Series of Suggestions

We cross the Tigris
on a floating bridge
snapping pictures
of the remains:
blasted concrete pillars
and the road they carried.

Decades earlier, Major Majid
ferried his new wife
across the same river
in his friend's fishing boat.
When I ask about bridges,
that's what he remembers.

As we pull back
onto the road,
our driver laughs, *What*
were you photographing?
The body
was on the other side.

I live between
different heats.
Distance is a constant
suggestion. Upheaval, too.
Syria, Iran, Turkey,
the black flag,
cholera, secession.

But mulberries are ripe
as I leave Iraq. Mulberries
ripe as I arrive in the States.
Walking, I pick a few
to eat there, on the sidewalk, by
the honeysuckle, yellow jasmine.
I pinch the stamen and pull
until a single bead
hangs at the opening. I hold
the open flower steady
and sip.

My brother and I married into a single family. Two families just changed daughters. No one had to pay the dowry. It is a common practice. I had no wedding party. I didn't go to a salon. I combed my hair, put the veil on, and went to his house. That was it. I was just a girl in a house and then we were married.

Our children? We gave them big parties. Drums, dancers, speakers, singers. Okra, goat meat in a summer red sauce or a winter white. Now, we can't do this. If we had anything, I'd make lunch for you. But then, I'm not on my feet much these days. The blood pressure.

I used to be a housewife. We had five sons and three daughters. All our children had their own rooms. Then, they all got married and had children of their own, and suddenly our house wasn't big enough! By the time we left, there were no other houses standing. We had lived beside Christians, Kurds, Shabak. We had all lived as one hand. Daesh separated us. The bombing. The shrapnel.

My son's wife, I hoped she would be the first in our family to finish middle school. But Daesh stopped that. My family didn't allow me to go to school. My father was a laborer. My mother sold the milk from our cows. My brothers were mechanics and truck drivers. They were backward and close-minded, and I sent all my grandchildren to school. I would have loved to be a doctor. Or anyone.

—Hamda

Khizr Camp, Mosul Province

Hamda's husband interrupts, "If this is an interview, ask her if she loves me."

Hamda rolls her eyes and says to me, "Of course I love him."

Her husband grins and, as he slips out between the tent flaps, says, "Kiss my eyes, sweetheart."

Hamda grins at me after he's gone. "I do love him."

I have lived my whole life in rented homes, moving from place to place. I moved five times before the Islamic State came and twice during that government. I loved the one house with a garden. We had oranges, roses, grapes. We played at our neighbors', at Um Nabeel's. She always assisted with the births. She was the person who told my father he had a daughter. Her husband, Abu Wisam, would always give people money when they had need. When the Islamic State came, they couldn't leave their house: they were Christian. I am a Muslim. There is no difference. We bought them groceries. Then, the terrorists took Abu Wisam's house and everything in it. My uncle helped them escape. I am half Kurd, half Arab. There is no difference.

That neighborhood had great shops for clothes and shoes. My mom has such good taste. She always bought me clothes. I could walk to school. There was a teacher there who beat my sister and me. So, we moved. At the next school, our teachers beat us. We had no father. I liked learning, but teachers kept hitting me. Students teased me for being well dressed. I didn't quite finish middle school. I had surgery and had to stay home. Then, the Islamic State came and there was no school.

Mosul was beautiful, especially the woods. That's where we would picnic before my father died. Near the waterfalls. My father always took us on picnics as children. The day he died, he was supposed to take us on one. He went to sell a car with his friends. There was an accident. He flew from the car and hit his head on a stone.

I like to watch movies at home. Horror movies. Anything with Michael Jackson. Once, my mother and I went on vacation in Erbil. We got lost in the mall. When we finally found our way out, we just went to our bus and stayed there. I won't be an immigrant. I love my city. But Mosul is a ghost town. I visited Mosul a month ago—at night—and I was so scared to get a cab that I was shivering. We went back fifteen days ago, for my grandfather's funeral, and there was a bombing in the middle of the house.

I didn't have a childhood like others. I'm sorry I'm crying. When my father died, my grandfather didn't let us live in the house. He forbade us a childhood. When he died, I wasn't sad. He didn't love me. Don't worry about saying you're sorry.

—Haneen
Khizr Camp, Mosul Province

In the 1980s, there was no internet, Facebook, video games, playgrounds. We got to dream. We all dreamed of a bike. When people all have cars, what's there to dream about? I had dreams I couldn't make real. I wanted to go to the US and learn English. If you learn that, all other things open to you. I wanted to go to the White House, where all the decisions are handed out. I would like to go to a real stadium. I want to see a game. Paris. Istanbul.

When I was young, I played. Soccer. I became a coach. I coached the village team for years. In the city they had many teams. In the village we had only enough players for a final match. One game, and we had our champions. Sure, I had a favorite player on the team: Acra Majid. He was a joker. I could play him anywhere. If I put him in, we would win. He was like Carl Lewis.

I saw him on TV. 1984. The Olympics. My family would go to sleep and I'd stay up. Before 1980, we had no power, no hot water, no pavement. We used candles. TV came with power. But black and white! No color. I loved football—American football. The pads! The fighting! The face paint!

I swam for fun. All the children swam. You know, teaching a child to swim is like scratching a stone. We would learn to swim in summer, when the water was low, and then we could swim year-round. We would go to the cinema. Action movies. Bruce Lee, Jackie Chan. Another man who could get hit many times and still stand, but could knock out many men with one punch. We played 21. We played dominoes. We read.

After school, I would go to the Mosul City Library. I would check out books. There were so many books! And it was so organized. When I asked for a book, they could bring it to me. Mutannabi is my favorite. He has a line, something like, *It is shameful to do something and yet leave it undone.* I will never forget that. And, *You can't do all you wish. The ship depends on the wind.* Mutannabi is home. And they say, *East or west! Home is best.*

—Majid
Khizr Camp, Mosul Province

Before sunrise, I'd start milking. The children would play with the animals, following them around. Milking is a gentle thing. In the spring, you milk twice a day. If the animal has given birth, only once. In winter, you do not milk at all. I was healthy. My children were young. So, I did the work.

I loved to cook yogurt because my family loved to eat it. Every morning, I would put the fresh milk on a fire, bring it to a boil, and reduce it to a simmer. After a while, I would take it off the heat and cover it with a towel. A couple hours later, it's ready. Eat that once and you'll never get enough of it. You'll stop eating canned food and boxed yogurt. These kids run around for a candy bar, but they don't know about true sour cream.

What the family couldn't eat, we would take to a village shop to sell. Everyone in the village was family: cousins, my husband's brothers and sisters. My whole life: family. Before we married, I had known my husband my entire life. I was seventeen when he gave my mother the gold. I was twenty when I had my first son. The other three came almost every year after.

I have three brothers and no sisters. When I see others with their sisters, I get jealous. Sisters visit you. My eldest brother is a barber; my middle brother, a contractor; my youngest, a logger. I didn't finish elementary school. It is part of our tradition: girls do not go to school after twelve or thirteen. That's how we live. We did not get to go to university. Boys did. From my family, I'm the only one who kept animals. I hated to leave our animals. I took picture after picture with our animals—for the memories. This is the first time I have ever left home.

—Hanna
Haji Ali Camp, Mosul Province

Her daughter crawled onto my lap. Some camp sickness crusted around her nostrils. She wouldn't stop touching my pen as I wrote, as her mother spoke. Down the page, like a heartbeat registering on a monitor, you could see where the little girl had reached out to touch the pen. Hanna kept apologizing. *She's never seen a woman write before.* When the little girl sneezed, nestled between my arms and the notebook, I simply used my sleeve. Hanna rushed to apologize. Then, I asked the best way to milk a goat. Hanna's aunts and grandmothers, seated around us, dozing in the tent, suddenly interrupted. They brought imaginary bowls to hold between their feet, arguing as they showed me how to properly tend their imaginary goats. Hanna grinned. No one apologized.

Nahla: I'm half Kurd and half Arab. My mother was a housewife. My father was an officer in the Iraqi army. I went to school until fifth grade. None of the girls behind you have the right to go to school. Our tribe is uneducated. None of the girls go to school.

Lam': All the women behind you are my grandchildren. I raised five sons and a daughter. My father was a village sheikh, like my husband. In the 1980s, like many others, I went to adult school. I learned to write my name, my father's name. I even learned some verses of the Qur'an.

I forgot all my good memories. I don't even remember last week. I did learn how to read and write.

I remember our home. People say that Kurds and Arabs were enemies, but that's not true. Their happiness was our happiness. We didn't even have water in the house.

We had electricity, water, gardens. Two sheep that took care of themselves.

We kept five hundred sheep.

I loved to cook okra.

Yes, okra.

The Sheikh and I, our fathers are friends. I knew him before the wedding night. I didn't stay enough in the city to achieve my dreams. I wanted to become a doctor, but in the villages, girls can't go to the schools.

I was sixteen years old. He asked for my hand. I got married. It was fate. I had no dreams. We met on our wedding night.

For fun? Henna nights. We make our henna. We light candles. We dance. We put water in the henna and make a paste until the color deepens. We color our legs, our hands, the palms of our hands. That was our only beauty. But it wasn't just beautiful. It strengthened the skin after working with animals. Twice a week we slept with plastic bags over our hands, covered in henna. We covered our hair, too, to keep it from falling out. I would henna my hair, down to the roots and the scalp, every six hours because my hair was so thin.

The circumcisions were fun, too. We would circumcise the child, then ululate. We threw chocolate on the child's head. We slaughtered a goat. We fasted. We prayed. Our sons and daughters came to visit. The whole family gathered. In a village, there is no place for women in a mosque. Women don't go. Men go. There are no women's rights. We can't finish our education. Even a female parliamentarian came on TV and said men should be allowed to marry many wives.

The houses? The entire village was destroyed. We hope the United States comes to see this destruction. We had grown. Now, there are twenty-five people in this tent. My husband and I rent a house.

Mosul is our city. Is there something more beautiful than Mosul? Mosul was our city.

Iraq was vulnerable, sure, but we didn't cause this.

I can't say more. I saw the same thing. I have the same story.

—Lam', fifty-six years old, first wife
—Nahla, thirty-nine years old, second wife
Haji Ali Camp, Mosul Province

A guard sticks his head into the tent and asks, “Are you talking about the old man?” Nahla looks away from the interview to say, “What old man? We’re talking about our lives.”

Before I married my wife, I was in love with another. In the summer, we would work in the fields. That's when I saw her. Love at first sight. She worked her family land. I worked mine. Tomatoes. Watermelon. We planted, watered, and harvested side by side. It was a pure love. I was twenty years old. I was in university. I asked her family for her hand. They said, *You are a stranger. You are not our relative. No.* This tribal structure is a problem. The man her family gave her to was old. Uneducated. But that's how it goes here.

Then, my family found a woman for me. She could barely write her name. We went to see her. She came in from the fields. Her face, her dress: right from the fields. She brought the tea, and I said to myself, *She's OK for me.*

Our villages were separated by the river. A river between us and no bridge. I said, *How will I make a party for her? For her family?* I went to my friend who had a fishing boat, my friend named Friday, and we married on a Friday. We made dinner and we ate all together, by hand, digging in with our hands. How many dishes? Just the one. This was normal.

—Majid
Khizr Camp, Mosul Province

The Plains of Nineveh

Water tanks stand on stilts above the improvised dumping ground, semi-trucks pass goats grazing in the median. Broken blast barriers and eucalyptus choke the river, which swirls with motor oil sheen. A guardhouse stands on a berm. The land beneath it is green with grasses and herbs that make long-hanging meat taste fresh, even fried. This is the season of narcissus, wild and delicate, growing into the miles of trenches the Islamic State dug. Villagers will cut the narcissus in handfuls and take it to the city, standing at intersections, asking 1,000 dinars–75 cents–for each. Drivers will stop a moment, buy a bunch, and carry it throughout the day, giving each person they meet a few stems until the bouquet is gone. Today, the oil wells the Islamic State set on fire as they retreated burn on. The streets of Qayyarah run crude. The oil is so black it could reflect the sky, if the smoke didn't cloud so low, rising from the plains like foothills.

The responsibility is so old I don't remember when it started. We open our home. We are the hotel, the refuge. We never eat alone. We host people upon people. We resolve disputes. We built the mosque that houses the only elementary school we have. In my family, we always said, *Gathering is learning.* Sitting with people is a kind of school. You learn from them as from a teacher. Generations of our family, as they have come and gone, keep the message: Be generous. Value peace. Be a house of the prophets, history, culture, reason.

We encourage patience, courtesy, negotiation. Even when our family doesn't have enough, we host others. Give and give with no thought for how much you have. We are one family. Strangers are family. My grandfather never ate dinner before ten in his life: he would wait, collecting guests for dinner, until the last train left town.

What do I mean by patience? Well, my grandson got hit by a motorcycle. His head split open. He needed seventeen stitches. We didn't say, *We will hunt your child now.* It was an accident. We took our child to the hospital. Another example? A stray bullet hit my nephew. Two men had a fight. It was an accident. We did not shoot their nephew. We are mostly peaceful people. Fools start fights. Wise men resolve the problem when it is still small.

Mosul once held all communities, all minorities. Our city of peace. The Mother of Two Springs. Nineveh. Mosul. So many names. When Daesh held Mosul, the bombings were constant. We went underground, but the birds I kept couldn't go anywhere. I had Chinese chickens, cockatiels, lovebirds, pigeons, finches. Before Daesh, I had fifty-eight lovebirds. Just lovebirds. I would put my open hand into their cage and couldn't close it for all the lovebirds that would land. When Daesh began to retreat from

Mosul, they set our oil wells on fire. No one knows how to put the fires out, so the oil wells burn and the air turns black. The smoke stunted trees and killed the last of my birds.

Now, I come to this room to sit, surf Facebook, be alone. Do you have Facebook? We could be friends. I charge my laptop and my phones. I smoke cigarettes. I love to smoke shisha. I know. A sheikh who smokes shisha. Baghdad engineers helped me design this room, but the portable burner, the storage for coffee cups, the ashtray: I made those by hand. The past few years, we couldn't leave the house or work, so I kept myself busy making these things. They have no name. Sometimes a thing has no name, but it's pretty. These pots for brewing, steaming, and pouring coffee are over a hundred years old. They are always clean: they are always boiling.

—Sheikh Abdul-Razak
Qayyarah, Mosul Province

I relate the story to a friend, a colleague in the field. She misunderstands why I've told the story. She says, *Yes, interpreting is tricky. Perhaps he said "forbearance." Maybe even "long-suffering."*

I think of the woman who sat beside me for that interview. A young Êzîdî woman nervous to be among Arabs, to be that close to Daesh, having only narrowly survived Shingal a couple years before. She had never interpreted, but spoke Arabic. I wanted to give her work. She wanted to work.

Interpreting lives in the instant. A word will suddenly come to you days or weeks after a conversation. So, you use *patience* when it's not quite *patience*. So, a student of mine says, *Fighting with swords isn't fighting*. So, I thought I was saying, *forgive, confess, disappoint, leave,* when I was saying, *free their neck, tread on your teeth, break my hands, carry my head*. So, I learned: when someone puts me above their eyes, I put them above my head. I learned to shatter the sugar.

Time helps, but not always. I once read *Mount Tur* and spent weeks searching out the meaning: *Radish Mountain*! A merciful few days later, sharing the translation with a dear friend, a devout Muslim, he laughed. *I thought you knew this mountain. I know you know this mountain. Moses's mountain.* I am misreading mountains.

A village tradition few city girls keep: the women boil grain sugar with perhaps cinnamon, maybe walnuts, and pour it into sheets to cool. The women aim the handles of their minute hammers against the sweet sheets as if against a pane of glass to make the first breaks, then turn the hammers' head against the lips of specially carved bowls built to ease this smaller breaking. This way, they make rock candy their guests will hold, one rough-spun sliver at a time, on their tongues as they sip their tea. And so, "to shatter the sugar" has come to mean "to flatter" or even "to shoot the shit."

The woman who taught me how to sip tea with shattered sugar on my tongue, she gave me the first ripe raw fig I'd ever eaten. She peeled it for me, to show me how Kurds approach the fruit. She put her hand on my arm, leaned in, and lovingly told me I did have a bit of a mustache and we would take care of it. She taught me the word for raisin, *kishmish*: a sound that so delighted me, I attempted my first joke in the new language. *I'll name my first child this*, I said. *God forbid*, she said, grinning around her sugar, sipping at her tea. Years later, translating a centuries-old poem, I stumble on the epithet *sugar-breaker* and see her.

Briefly Home

Pupils wide as plates
I wash my brain
fold by fold
in the kitchen sink
until I can smile
again effortlessly.
They stroke my cheek
and say, *Will you be gone*
tomorrow? The muscles
hadn't atrophied.
It was the ill use
that hurt.
The clouds were giant boots
until they were a wisp
of a person
I loved very much
and recognized.
Don't worry about the vomit.
I'm not.

Drought

After the day's last call to prayer
there is no external marker of night passing,
only me, alone, slowly turning to water.

The evening helps me out of my skin,
as if out of a taxi or a coat,
and all that was contained,
all that I held together,
I let loose. Still,

I could throw
all the water
I am
at the desert below
and not be enough
for a sapling.

I wish I could spend my life
as a brain in a jar.

I put a tomato in my mouth.
I test its skin,
how breakable, how spillable
everything is inside.
I love the sudden water
of the skin pulling back.
I hate the breaking and
I love the water.

Time stopped. Stopped. Color stopped. We kept our secrets in our basements. We forgot things, and when we remembered, it hurt.

When they first searched my house, they had no flashlights. But I knew they'd come back. I ran to the garden and buried my violin. They didn't find the violin, but they still took me. My father didn't know the violin was there. He watered the garden. I hoped a little violin flower would grow up, even become a cello with time.

Driving home, ISIS stopped me, searched the car, found the guitar, and shattered it. They shot three bullets off beside my ear. I thought I was dead. Then, they stabbed me. It's OK. It wasn't a big stab. OK, any stab is a big stab, but really, it was a small stab. They just wanted to scare me. That was my first guitar.

I lived as a Moslawi. I suffered as a Moslawi. I sang in the deepest rooms of my house. The suffering was years: a project of ending life, slowly ending life. My age is young. Nothing else is.

My second guitar, the one I still play today, I stowed in a rice bag. There was no one to teach me. The internet was so expensive. So expensive. One hour of bad internet was 7,500 Iraqi dinars. I could download the piece I wanted to play, no tutorials. There were no teachers. There was anger. I had to feel anger. In music, there was anger and more. I could play what I couldn't say. In those years, no one could speak to anyone, no one could understand anyone. I needed to bring soul to death.

—**Awtar Nergal**
Mosul

That day, four ISIS snipers took the Kirkuk Palace, the most famous hotel in Kirkuk, which is not a hotel anymore. You know, everyone in Kirkuk had a gun, so before the Asayish or pesh merga could engage, people did. And it was a mess, bullets everywhere, so stupid.

After a couple hours, three snipers had been shot and the fourth jumped to his death. People dragged the bodies from the hotel out into the streets, through the streets, finally hanging the bodies in a butcher shop window, as a warning.

When war comes home, whatever you do, you don't think about humanity. You think any defense of your home is dignity itself. But children saw this.

The same thing happened in Fallujah: civilians, police, dragging the bodies of ISIS fighters behind their cars, street after street. I have video of it. You rethink everything in times like these. Is what we do different from ISIS? Any one of us, after we do something like this, can be ISIS. That mind is in all of us. Somehow.

—Hawre Khalid
Slemani

But children saw this.

Mamosta Mullah Ahmad Qazi was my first teacher. Before he would preach or teach, he would lean his Kalashnikov, like a walking stick, against the wall. Then, education would go like this: the teacher would give a lesson and instruct us to memorize it. Two days later, we would recite the lesson from memory. On recitation days, the teacher would have his shepherd's crook in hand, ready to beat us if we hadn't learned our lesson. On recitation days, students would wear thick clothing, so the cane wouldn't hurt so badly when it struck. Once, a teacher hit a boy so hard, his head flew into the classroom window and bled. Then, I saw the teacher see himself and pause. As a second grader, I knew the names of the months. In front of all the students, that teacher asked me to recite the months. I did. The students clapped for me. He asked others to do the same. None could. He told them they could clap for themselves with their fingernails.

—**Ali Bapir**
Hawler

There was a donkey in my village, all the children tortured him. He grew so tired, he ran away from the village and into the mountains, into the trees. There, he found a lion, dead. He took the skin and shrugged it over himself. Then, he came home to the village. Everyone was terrified of him and treated him with respect. He thought, *If the skin worked so well, I will roar. How much more will they fear and respect me then?* But when he opened his mouth, he could only bray. So, the villagers understood the trick and the donkey lost his skin.

—Ali Bapir
Hawler

Going into the interview, a friend says, *Be careful with that one. He's slippery.*

What does that mean? I ask, but he won't say more.

A politician, an Islamic conservative, a jihadist. He tells me of his youth, how he hoped to show Americans he was peaceful. He brought American journalists to the encampment. They spent the day. He drove them back. That night, as he drove, special forces hit. A precision strike. He alone lived because he wasn't there to die.

When he begins to cry, I am not sure if it's shameful. I place the fresh handkerchief I always carry in winter on the table and remove my hand. I don't look at him. I hear him pick it up, dab at his face; I see the white square laid down.

I realize I am the first American he has spoken to since. I look so much like a journalist. I pick up the handkerchief and use it myself.

But months before, I didn't ask how they knew the body in the river was ISIS.

After all the children all those parents had put in my arms, after they misunderstood what kind of doctor I was–children with botched amputation sites, eyes crusted into blindness with who knew what, skin blotched with burns that wouldn't heal or sloughing off from bathing in putrid water–I had been content to see the body in the river so bloated.

It seemed right. In fact, it felt good. Like justice.

That mind is in all of us. Somehow.

Teaching

At the market, the pomegranates lie, spread wide, on the carts. Not a seed loose, tight ruby honeycomb. If I had the Kurdish, I would ask how they part the calloused skin, how they make the fruit fall open.

Instead, I watch the men work their knives: with a quick stroke, they circle the crown, the pucker where the flower grew and fell. Their thumbs gentle on the knife's back, they trace the fruit's longitude, teaching the skin where to break.

What's Wild

The street is bright:
pomegranates, oranges, carrots,
sour apples, shining locks linked in long chains,
moneychangers' tightly banded rainbows.

Small teaspoons ring
like thin tin clappers
in the narrow-waisted bells
of glass cups.

At the bridge, stairs lead under,
where the animal sellers sit.
Business is slow. They cut boxes
to fit cage bottoms.

In a plastic tub, intestines:
fresh, sleek, dark, coiled,
and loud with light. Hunger
makes the ravens intent.

One pigeon is tethered: her leg on a string.
The man selling her is proud. Her tufted ankles catch
the wind and lift her up and over. She flips and flips and,
tangled, falls back into his hands. The seller, a mountain man
like them all, knows which teeth to pull to lizard the snake.
As he pulls at the pigeon's knots, he says, *What's wild has rights.*

Omar and the Hoopoe

Omar explains: the hoopoe has a special bone
        that will grant a woman what she wants
        if she carries it with her. So, she buys the bird,
with its expressive crest,

she butchers and boils,
        waits for the first bone to float up:
        that she rescues.

Omar likes the bird for its purity. The Qur'an made it sacred.
        He likes it, too, because when it raises its head feathers,
        like a peacock, it looks like a teenage boy with gelled hair—
experimenting, trying for handsome, arriving at surprised.

The bird, perhaps,
        makes him think of his son,
        who comes to the market one day
dressed in mock fatigues

with the Kurdish sun stitched onto the hat.
        Omar places his arm around his son's shoulders
        and asks for a picture. He himself soldiered
for twenty-one years, first with one army, then another.

He's free now,
        has the key to his own shop.
        But in this country, a man has only three options:
get kicked, live in sorrow, or run.

Nothing is permanent,
        nothing punctual,
        not even his soldier's pension.
He says you could throw all Iraqis—

Sunni, Shia, Kurd—
        into the hottest fire
        and never melt them down.

You Gave

You gave the lie a mouth
so it loved you
and stayed
Shouting at it
only made it giddy
No one had ever
spoken to it before

You were better than a mirror
better than a reflection
You were a body
built like a sparrow
to bear and be marked by
every idea the lie
could load
onto you
It adored you

but gave you nothing

And when the lie returns
(it always does
you're the only home it's ever known)
its adoration will be anger
its emptiness will sound like accusation
Don't argue
There is no reassurance
no love enough
for a lie

There is no way
to rid yourself
of a lie only

stop giving
it your mouth

The Road Was Closed

I.

The road was closed
But the guards had been students
of a teacher who was with us
so we drove on
The road was closed
so it was empty
and the dead men
no one had moved them
because they had stood
in life with men
of the black flag
Someone would salvage
their trucks but the dead men
would rot maybe find a river
and bloat past
recognition into
fish food How many
people will eat the fish
How many people
will get sick like this
The road was closed
and who were we
to the militias who patrolled it
so we drove as fast as we could
among the craters
the landscape made military
We drove so fast

the young man in the back seat
leaned forward Gently he said
Dr my mother loves me
The driver the Dr laughed
He had driven tanks
the army the war the draft
If a man must die the Dr said *he should*
die like a mountain
The road was closed at every checkpoint
We drove home
but the road was closed

II.

We had set out to see Hatra
the city known as the house of gods
where all gods were welcome
another vision of Mosul
before the black flag
aside from the black flag
The road was open
but no one could understand
why we wanted to travel it
gaping chunks gone
where IEDs had been sown
The road was open but the
shadowed flag still flew Another
road a dirt road had been driven
into the shoulder Each car crossing
Nineveh's plains coughed out
small cyclones of dust

In a city of rivers only one bridge
remained a one-lane floating
bridge the Americans had left
behind Each day half the city
spent half the day waiting in
traffic to reach the other side

The Hashd soldier at the checkpoint
cut his commander's hair
with school scissors
better used on construction paper
The road was open
he told us still cutting
but the bridge had been taken
somewhere else
Sure sure we laughed and drove on
And the bridge was gone
So we drove back
And the soldier laughed
Have you ever seen a Hashd lie

The bridge was gone
so we stopped by a roadside shop
for raisin juice dark and velvet
thick and light with mint
spring becoming summer
served in drinking bowls

We took another road
that the man known
as the Goddess's Nanny
remembered as leading to Hatra
A Hashd outgrown by his machine gun
looked up from Facebook
What do you want with this road he said
We are going to see Hatra we said
What is Hatra he said
Sit on a bottle
our driver the Dr said

after the windows were up
and we were down the road a ways

We are four kilometers from Hatra
but this commander at this checkpoint
hasn't heard a thing
about us or visitors or us
Thieves and sons of thieves
the Dr says
when we are finally
turned away out from under
their mounted guns

Every road was open
but we could not get to Hatra

III.

At the Baghdad museum:

A woman in the pose of worship
A woman at suckle
A Lady Sky
The goddess in different positions

STOLEN AND RETURNED
AFTER THE EVENTS OF 2003

Paving stones
from the Temple of Sin
depict the God of Animals
a lion cub in the crook of his arm

STOLEN AND RETURNED
AFTER THE EVENTS OF 2003

A plaque reads
detonated   no
decorated

The Gods of Wind and Wisdom broke
though curators lined the galleries
with sandbags to soften their fall
to break the impact of a bomb
Someone inscribed a bird
with incantations to prevent
the fear and panic of children

STOLEN AND RETURNED
AFTER THE EVENTS OF 2003

A priest with wide eyes
hair of snails
robes falling from his shoulders
like so many languid violins
has his right hand
raised still in greeting

HATRA 312-139 BC

Next to him Hercules stands
both thighs inscribed
one with Aramaic
one with Latin
his cock cradled
between two languages
two alphabets

HATRA 312-139 BC

Beside him, one woman rides
while another leads her forward
with a raised tambourine

HATRA 312-139 BC

Hatra everywhere
At eye level a cunt curls
between the thighs
of Naked Woman Reclining
With Nursing Child
The spirits above lean toward
one another
listening
one breathes
into a flute

HATRA 312-139 BC

Women in burqas
walk below

All those Hatras
no one is prepared to find

Glass Tangerine

The moon stayed with us
the whole morning,
bright and full and unashamed
in the daylight.

We swam our makeshift course
across the vast lake and back.

On our drive home, snacking
on dates, Nab tells me
how he never really learned
to swim, how he only
wanted to see the seagulls
hatch, how afraid he was.

He said, *You know, we say, I broke my fear.*

That glass tangerine
we carry carefully
for years.

Hanoosi

I am your nightingale. A little jumpy thing you call Hanoosi. When you ask me to kiss you, I peck your ear. When I see how much my kiss pleases you, I pull at your lobe with my beak. We play hide-and-seek on the table's edge. I know the sound of your horn in the driveway. I know how to dive at your daughters to drive them from you. To make more space in your hands for me. I am Hanoosi. And you make my life walk.

Worship

You are not any of the names I have for you.
How can I call you?

The call to prayer comes. You answer.
What kind of lover waits to be called?

The cave is empty. The city is full.
You have wrapped your tongue
around sound
in a place where there is no echo.
Come here. Speak.

You say you believe
in constant prayer.
Come here.

Dream State

The boys fly kites.
Tomato paste cans for spools.
Cotton sewing thread for the line.
Plastic bags splayed across twigs for the kite.
Every time a kite comes down, a boy fixes it.
Yusuf has flown his all the way to the next village.
Across electricity lines!
Ibrahim, Yusuf's brother, says, *If we had*
just one more plastic bag,
we would make one for you.

Khizr Camp to the airport.
Slemani to Istanbul. Istanbul to Colombo.
Deep night   nothing open   heat so thick
the mosquito netting traps it against the bed.

A train calls from where the tracks parallel the coast.
            But no more trains run here.
                                        They've torn down the platforms,
torn up the tracks that ran through the fields where a little boy once stood,
working the fields with his family, crying and waving to the departing
passengers he didn't know, unable to understand what departure was.

A dog barks.   Barks.   Barks.   Yes, that is a dog.

Rhythmic male chanting distends
over a loudspeaker.   Not the call to prayer.   Too late, too
choral   and this is Buddhist country.
Tuktuks and buses with their quickstep trumpets.   A dog barks.

A bell rings six times   but doesn’t signal the hour.

A flatbed sells vegetables and fruits, but not stove-bound gas canisters, no “Für Elise” alerting customers in their homes, no “Für Elise” distorted by two megaphones duct-taped to the driver’s-side mirror.

The chant continues. A pigeon coos, *Oh no! Oh no! Oh no!*

I’m falling asleep beside Borges. His dreamtigers are my dreaming tiger, there at the foot of the bed, breathing heavily. I fit myself in beside them and curl around them in the little light.

When I turn to sleep, our spines settle against each other.

We listen to the foghorns outside make their accidental chords. I think of the men who call a city to prayer and their chorus, distorted by loudspeakers, stretched across the cityscape, their voices bashing into each other before the thought of dawn. How many of the callers still climb the stairs? How many of the calls are recordings, a button pressed by some sleepy servant of the prayer rug?

Borges is interested. He asks if I’ve found out any more about those sister-wives of the last prince of the Ardalans.

I forgot. I can’t believe I forgot to tell you. Yes, they were both poets.

You should write about it.

It feels like you already have.

Revelations

And the kings of the earth, and the great men, and the rich men, and the chief captains, and the mighty men, and every bondsman, and every free man, hid themselves in the dens and in the rocks of the mountains; and said to the mountains and rocks, *Fall on us, and hide us from the face*. And the mountains laughed low and the rocks caught the joke and their laughter grew and shook the men down into the deserts, where even the sand laughed and would not swallow them up.

So the men stood on the dust and looked at one another broken to shivering, and there was none to take pity on them, not even one another, and nowhere else to look in the long, empty horizon, except to one another.

And after these things, I saw four angels standing on the four corners of the earth, holding the four winds of the earth, that no wind should blow on the earth, the sea, or any tree. And another angel descended, crying with a loud voice to the four angels, to whom it was given to hurt the earth and sea, *Hurt not the earth, neither the sea, nor the trees, till we have sealed the servants in their forehead.*

And when they had opened their forehead and the trumpets had faded, I saw the great procession unbroken–peripatetic on earth, your home is their forehead—and in the great procession walked children trailing handmade kites spooled on tomato paste cans and children trailing their severed hands and their mothers and fathers behind them carrying their own heads that had long since fallen off and sisters and brothers who tried to pick the heads clean of sticks and leaves and gravel from where the heads had rolled along on the ground before anyone could catch them.

And at the head of the procession, entering the forehead first, was the man and woman whose child had died on the first days of the walk and rested in his arms, then hers, then back again, but always dead.

And the men in the desert plains were leaden and could not walk.

And the men in the desert plains could only watch.

And the men in the desert plains were made to watch.

And to the men in the desert plains came each name of each who walked, and each name uttered echoed infinitely even as each who walked blinked out of sight into the seal of their forehead.

And the men desired to die and death laughed, light-footed.

And the men sought death and death winked, winked again, and winked out.

And all their tears called the scorpions whom they had made thirsty and the scorpions' sternums were breastplates and their book lungs were stacked spears and the scorpions laughed with death, both with the faces of men, so the men in the desert plains would recognize the creatures, and recognize each woe waiting for them behind the first.

And death could rest while the scorpions went to work.

And death could weep for no one was found worthy to open and to read the book.

And a creature crept up and placed her head under death's hand and whined and grinned until death understood and gave to the creature the book. And the creature read from the book, and the creature read the world it had always wanted.

And the words came to the walkers like honey, and the walkers sipped and sipped at the words, and their bellies distended, for this was their first food in too long, and still they sipped for the words were good, even when bitter, and sped their way.

And the way they tread began to speak, for the words sifted through their blood, strengthening their bones until they overflowed, and the way began to guzzle the word.

And the way spoke for the olive trees, which were groves, and the way praised those who had left the olive groves unburned even in the course of war, and the way praised those who again left the olive groves unburned even as the war closed, and the trees bore the marks of those the trees and their gentle heights had helped to hang, and the way praised those who learned to eat once more from those trees who had been shaken, untimely shaken, shaken bare of unripe fruit, and shaken had learned to fruit once more.

The way was generous and the olive grove was brave and the olive grove was braver than many of the hands who touched her, but not all.

And the olive grove gave power to the tent camp, which arose and shook off its dust in a great billowing cloud, and the tents, out of their mouths, spewed fires that spoke as one, saying, *We have shut heaven. As we stand, so we have shut heaven.*

And the men in the desert plains made their blood water, to put out the fires, but the fires consumed them, and remained thirsty, though the men became a great flood.

And each leaden corpse the dried-out men became was like unto a headstone.

And the headstones fell into place like pavement.

And the pavement smoothed the way through the desert for those still walking on foot.

And the walkers began to sing and give thanks, for the way was good and the way was clear and the way was death.

And the walkers laughed with death, who was the way, and the walkers laughed with the way.

And the way and death laughed with them, who were their friends.

And there appeared a great wonder above: a woman small though big with child, gripped by suffering.

And there appeared another wonder above: a beast of teeth, ready to devour the child as soon as it was born.

And the woman fled to the wilderness and the wilderness sheltered the woman and the wilderness fed the woman.

And the woman did not stop her eating until she was wilderness.

And the wilderness revealed itself to the beast, whose many teeth found purchase, and the beast glutted itself on the wilderness, and none prevailed.

For the beast had eaten the wilderness whole.

And the wilderness grew and the woman grew within the wilderness and her baby within her.

And the beast slept, sated.

And the woman brought forth the child into the wilderness, and they split the beast from the belly, and the beast of teeth recognized the woman and the child who were formed, white as the bleached bones of wilderness.

And the woman laid hands on the beast as it bled and stuffed the trumpets as they rang with rags.

The child wailed, and the woman alongside the child, for the beast had been a wonder, undone by hunger; for their freedom was a terror.

And the child learned to hold terror, and the child's hands grew strong with terror, and the woman knew not how to hold her freedom, which was terror, and the wilderness called again to the woman, who fled again into it.

And the wilderness helped the woman, and the wilderness opened up her mouth, and swallowed up the terror, and belched, and the wilderness opened up her mouth, and the woman climbed her lip, and the wilderness yawned, and the woman stretched up to climb her teeth, and the wilderness slept, and the woman slept inside, and there was no more terror, and there was no more woman, only the wilderness asleep.

And the child rejoiced and tossed the terror hid in the child up to the sky, where it stayed, bright and burning like so many stars, like so much unripe fruit that could no more be shaken down by men out of season.

And the child knew and did not confess a name.

And the child was hurricane.

And the child was joy.

And I stood on hills of scree, clinging to half my name, inscribed on a pebble, and I saw the creature move, and I saw the creature see the child.

And fear for the child moved me, and still I could not cry out.

And the creature drew close to the child.

And the creature moved like a thief.

And the child inclined unto the creature, though the child was blind to the creature.

And my voice came to me like trumpets and I cried out to the child and the expanses of scree gave my voice back to me, relentlessly my cries were returned to me.

And the creature sniffed the child's ear. And the child giggled. And the creature sneezed and was charmed and laid itself beside the child and locked eyes with me and I heard the creature say, *Here is wisdom.*

And my keening became song, and my song was cities, and I sang so long I laid my head in Baghdad and my feet in the Pacific, and I rested in my new song that was Babylon and Mosul and Slemani and Duhok and highways that could lead to Syria and highways that could lead to Rojava and not one highway that could lead home, for highways cede to oceans.

And the song did not know home, or the song did not understand home, or the song was home, and so can never be homeless.

And this new song, even for the walkers, even for the procession, was enough.

And a walker stood out, perfumed in jasmine, and called me *Enough*. The walker named me with a loud cry and the walker inscribed my new name, *Enough*, which was *Abundance*.

And the walker walked on, into their forehead, and the walker's scent lingered, and jasmine was the walker's sign, and so it became mine, and so I am known among all the broken beer bottles and happy bullets, and so I am known in the citadels, and so my name is returned to me by the collapsing wells that once sustained the citadels, by the ruins of ruins that once held the dervishes of the citadels, so the marble tombs of saints, which actually hold saints, call back, *Abundance*.

For Nineveh swallowed its relics long ago.

For a name is the last relic left.

For the mystics who remain know only the most public name, and hold it dear, chanting with their echo-ridden cities, *No one but one, No one but one, No one but one*.

And the cities call back, *One, One, One*.

Until the name becomes new.

Until the name is *One*.

And the cities won't let me die, though they make my head loud with their cries.

And the waters and the earth refuse their help.

And the angels look, unmoved.

And wrath scorches me, like liver over live coals, but does not consume me.

And pain gnaws at me, but I am not supper.

And the river Euphrates laps at me, but does not sweep me away nor extinguish my smoking.

And the creature comes to me.

As one thief sees another, as thieves hear thieves, so I hear the creature.

And the creature knows I hear.

And the sky opens and my mouth is a sword, with which I cannot form an apology, and the creature lowers its head, and the creature turns its head, and all I see are apples, pink ladies, and all I can do is eat.

And the creature is not consumed, but tickled.

And my mouth is made new by its laughter.

And the creature names me *Child*.

And the creature calls me *Meat*. And the creature's mouth compasses me, and lying down, forepaws then haunches, the creature chews.

And the creature sees their forehead accept the last walker. And the creature sees their forehead accept death, who was peering in at the temples, hoping someone was still home. And the creature stands and shakes itself and surveys the world that has emptied and been made new, been made new and emptied,

And the creature begins to ring, like sea glass become crystal, and the creature becomes its song. And the song is set loose from the cities and their citadels, from wells and worship, from naming and from calling and from writing and from reading.

And the song dances over the ocean as if it were wind, though it is not.

And the song reaches the river, and flows like the river, though it is not one.

And the song flows upriver to the source.

And the source is above the eyes.

And the source welcomes the song, and the source is the song, and the song was the source, which the earth swallows and spews forth.

BIOGRAPHICAL INFORMATION

For every interview I conducted, I sought and received either verbal and recorded or written permissions from the interviewee. Each person I spoke with gave me permission to use their full name at the time, but as circumstances have evolved—and continue to evolve quite quickly—where it might contribute to someone's safety, I have used only first names.

Alana Marie Levinson-LaBrosse is a poet, translator, and assistant professor at the American University of Iraq, Sulaimani (AUIS). She was a 2022 NEA Fellow, the first ever working from the Kurdish, and serves as the Founding Director of Kashkul, a center for arts and culture at AUIS.

Ali Bapir is an Islamic thought leader and politician in the Kurdistan Region of Iraq. He founded and currently serves at the president of the Kurdistan Justice Group (previously the Islamic Group of Kurdistan). He fought as a pesh merga against Saddam Hussein's Ba'athist forces, survived the loss of dozens of his men at the hands of American soldiers in 2003, endured twenty-two months in one of Iraq's American prisons, and still to this day advocates for peaceful manifestations of devotion.

Awtar Nergal formed as a band during the Islamic State's occupation of Mosul. None of the members received classical training. Independently, each member of the band (Khaled al-Rawi on the oud, Hakam al-Zarari on the guitar, and Mohammed al-Adwani on the violin) reached for music however they could, risking their lives to play. When the Islamic State's occupation ended, Awtar Nergal was one of the first bands to perform publicly, bringing music back to the famously pluralistic city.

Halo Fariq is a translator. Having earned his BA in English literature in 2017, he immediately began translating between Kurdish and English. To date, he has translated thirty-nine books, including novels, poetry, graphic novels, and children's stories. His most recent translation was Yōko Ogawa's *The Memory Police.* He cofounded Befr, meaning "snow," a publishing house for translating, writing, and publishing children's books. Its primary target is to publish stories about the environment, climate change, and gender equality to help the next generation confront the world they receive. When he is not translating, editing, or reading, he serves as a major in the pesh merga.

Hamda, a mother and grandmother, was born and raised in Mosul. She worked tirelessly raising her children, supporting her grandchildren, and ensuring their education. The rise of the Islamic State interrupted her hopes for her first female relative to finish middle school. At the time of our interview, Hamda was living as an internally displaced person (IDP) with her extended family.

Haneen, along with her mother and her sisters, has navigated the world without the protection of male relatives. When her father died in a car accident, her grandfather abandoned his son's family. Instead of succumbing to despair, she built her own family with her neighbors, Christians and Kurds whom she and her mother then protected as the Islamic State swept into the city. At the time of our interview, Haneen was living as an IDP with her mother and sisters.

Hanna, a young mother, found peace among her flocks of animals. As her children were young, she tended her herds on her own, making products from their milk that she could sell throughout the village. At the time of our interview, Hanna was living as an IDP with her children, all under the age of ten, and her husband's extended family. Her journey to the IDP camp was the first time she'd ever left home.

Hawre Khalid is a Kurdish photographer from Kirkuk, one of Iraq's contested cities. He received his BA in journalism from Sulaimani University in 2007. He moved to the Netherlands for several years before moving back to Iraq, where he began his career as a photojournalist. He has since covered every aspect of the ongoing conflicts in Iraq. His work has been exhibited both in Iraq and Europe. Khalid regularly works with *The New York Times*, *Time* Magazine, *de Volkskrant*, Al Jazeera, *Der Spiegel*, and *The Sunday Time*, among others.

Lam' is the first wife of a village sheikh in Mosul Province. She asked that she be interviewed with her husband's second and decades-younger wife, Nahla. Lam' and Nahla sat side by side, in front of me, answering each question in their turn. Lam' had many children and grandchildren of whom she was so proud that she asked they be able to witness our interview. Even the littlest toddler sat quietly while the two women spoke except for once, when a boy who couldn't have been more than three crawled into Lam's lap for kisses and promises she would die for him, which she contentedly gave. At the time of our interview, in the middle of coalition forces wresting Mosul from Islamic State control, she and her whole family, including Nahla, lived as IDPs at the Haji Ali Camp.

Majid was the first person in his village to attend college. When we arrived early for our interview, he greeted us in a sweatsuit, apologized for his unkempt appearance, and came back twenty minutes later in a full suit and tie, the only formal clothes he salvaged from the ruins of his home after the Islamic State bombed it. His mustache had been brushed till it shone. He asked to be interviewed before we spoke to anyone else in the camp. We held all the correct official permissions, and still he gently insisted we interview him first, so he would have firsthand knowledge of what he was asking his people to experience. At the time of our interview, he ran Khizr Camp, an IDP camp established on the ruins of his old village.

Nahla is the second wife of a village sheikh in Mosul Province. She was asked by her husband's first wife, Lam', to be interviewed side by side, which she agreed to. She had no children. She wanted an education. She spoke freely. At the time of our interview, though the first wife of the family and all the descendants lived in Haji Ali Camp as IDPs, Nahla and her husband had a second home somewhere outside the camp, away from the family, where they lived.

Sheikh Abdul-Razak descends from generations of Qayyarah sheikhs who, throughout their tenure which extends before the town's collective memory begins, have provided a gathering place for storytelling, community meals, lodging for travelers, resources for those in need and have kept—and still sometimes do keep—the peace as both judge and jury. At the time of our interview, Sheikh Abdul-Razak was able to host me in his family's traditional home, which they had maintained as a shelter throughout the oppression of the Islamic State. We conducted our interview as a firefight between Islamic State and coalition forces broke out and died down a few blocks away and as the oil wells that the Islamic State had set on fire as they retreated burned on.

Sheikh Mohammed Ali Qaradaghi has worked as a mullah, preservationist, archivist, librarian, and prolific scholar. Throughout the course of his life, each of these disciplines has strengthened the others. Qaradaghi often accepted payment for Friday sermons in manuscripts; families would often approach Qaradaghi with manuscripts, asking him if he could find a place for them in his library, where the texts would be protected. Futhermore, he would publish on them as a scholar and bring them into the canon of Kurdish intellectualism. Qaradaghi served nine months in Saddam Hussein's prison for the then-crime of preserving Kurdish-language and Kurdish heritage texts. He has passed a love of culture on to his children and grandchildren. His son, Dr. Amjad Qaradaghi, a professor of architecture at the University of Sulaimani, developed the first Kurdish font in order to help his father digitize the collection.

Sheikh Yusuf Talabani serves as the spiritual leader of the Talabani Tekiye, a place where peripatetic scholars have come to rest, study, and exchange what some might even call heretical knowledge since the early nineteenth century. The tekiye, in its early days, birthed a region-wide revival of Qadiri Sufism, founded by Sheikh Abdul-Qadir Gilani in the eleventh century. Today, Sheikh Yusuf, his multilingual wife, Sheikha Sunbul, and their children carry on the family's legacy as thought leaders in their community. In the Talabani Tekiye, they ensure that men and women both serve as mullahs. The children choose their spiritual path; they are not indoctrinated. Adults affectionately send little ones home saying, "Go read a book!" They delight in celebrating within the worship all the languages present in the city: Arabic, Kurdish, Turkish, Turkmen, and Farsi. All are welcome, almost especially the stranger and the foreigner.

TERMS

Ardalans: a Kurdish princely family that governed in what is now northwest Iran from the early eleventh century until the mid-nineteenth century.

Asayish: the primary intelligence agency operating in the semiautonomous Kurdistan Region (KRI) of Iraq.

Chamchamali: Chamchamal is a town northeast of Kirkuk that falls within the borders of the KRI. Residents of Chamchamal, Chamchamalis, are known for their quick tempers and their habit of carrying guns. Kurdish people joke that Chamchamal is "the Texas of Kurdistan."

Daesh: a name, considered derogatory, for the Islamic State.

Erbil/Hawler: the capital city of the KRI, as many cities in Kurdish lands go by different names depending on who the speaker is. An Arab speaker will usually call the city "Erbil," where a Kurdish speaker will usually use "Hawler."

Hashd: an abbreviation of the Arabic name for what are known in translation as Popular Mobilization Units (PMU) or militias. To take back the city of Mosul from the Islamic State, many Hashd units arrived from Iran and then stayed. The tension between the newly liberated Sunni-majority Moslawi Muslims and the newly arrived Shia Hashd units was palpable.

Ijaza: the permission granted to a student from a teacher to teach a particular subject or text, usually within a religious context.

ISIS: an acronym for the Islamic State of Iraq and Syria.

Islamic State: an abbreviation of the full name for the Islamic State of Iraq and Syria (ISIS) or the Islamic State of Iraq and the Levant (ISIL).

Mamosta: the Kurdish word for "teacher," considered an honorific.

Moslawi: someone from Mosul.

Mullah: the common contemporary Kurdish latinization for a leader within the Muslim community, educated in Islamic theology and law.

pesh merga: Kurdish fighting forces.

Santur: a hammered dulcimer originating in Persia or Mesopotamia.
Shabak: a minority ethnic group of disputed origin living in the Nineveh Plains.

Sharia: Islamic law.

Sheikh: an honorific signifying an Arab leader; a village, family, or tribal chief.

Tekiye: a center for spiritual gathering, worship, and reflection that traditionally offered housing to peripatetic scholars of Islam, particularly Sufism.

YPG: an acronym for the People's Protection Units, majority-Kurd militias operating primarily in Syria that form the backbone of the Syrian Democratic Forces.

ACKNOWLEDGMENTS

"The Road Was Closed" appeared in *Urgencies = Insurgencies*, California Poets, vol. 1, edited by Forrest Gander and published by Nomadic Press (2020).

[The responsibility], [I have lived my whole life], [In the 1980s], [No one lives now], and [Before I married] appeared in *The Sewanee Review* (Winter 2018), originally titled "Patience," "Moving," "Childhood," "Education," and "Bridges."

"Glass Tangerine" appeared in *Bengal Lights* (November 2017).

"You Gave," originally titled "The Lie," appeared in *Epiphany* (Fall/Winter 2016).